American Presbyterianism.

A SERMON,

DELIVERED ON LORD'S DAY, NOVEMBER 11, 1853.

BY

GEORGE DUFFIELD, Jr.

American Presbyterianism.

A SERMON,

DELIVERED ON LORD'S DAY, NOVEMBER 11, 1853.

BY

GEORGE DUFFIELD, Jr.,

PASTOR OF THE COATES' ST. PRESBYTERIAN CHURCH.

"THE GLORY OF CHILDREN ARE THEIR FATHERS."—*Prov.* xvii. 6.

PUBLISHED BY REQUEST.

PHILADELPHIA:
PRINTED BY ISAAC ASHMEAD.
1854.

AMERICAN PRESBYTERIANISM.

"THE GLORY OF CHILDREN ARE THEIR FATHERS."—Prov. xvii. 6.

"HE is worthy for whom thou shouldst do this," said the Jews on one occasion to Jesus, "for he loveth our nation and hath built us a synagogue." Be it mine to show that the church, to-day for the first time making her appeal to her children, and whose cause I undertake to plead before you, is also worthy of assistance. The occasion is a sublime and a solemn one—1500 churches, and as many ministers, entering the gates of Zion, and making a simultaneous effort to extend the gospel to the destitute—this is the communion of saints indeed. Who is it that asks? and what is asked for? These are the points to which I would now invite your attention.

Eighty years after the arrival of the Mayflower at Plymouth, and twenty years after the landing of William Penn from the good ship Welcome at Coaquanock, a merchant sloop might have been seen entering the Capes of the Delaware. That sloop is to our denomination what the "Welcome" is to Pennsylvania, and the "Mayflower" to Massachusetts, and these United States. What Elder Brewster is to the Congregationalists, Roger Williams to the Baptists, Asbury to the Methodists, and Bishop White to the Episcopalians, FRANCIS MCKEMIE, the owner of that sloop, is to American Presbyterians.

While the little vessel, laden with the precious germ of all that we have since been as a church, is making her steady way to the newly constituted city of Philadelphia, let us indulge a very proper curiosity as to the man, by whose hand it has pleased God in his Providence to plant this germ. We shall find him in every way worthy of the honor that is thus conferred.

His native country is Ireland, where, at the early age of fourteen, he was converted to God through the instructions of a pious schoolmaster. Baptized in the Irish Presbyterian Church, and there educated and ordained, he early and deeply imbibed the enlarged and enlightened liberality of sentiment that prevailed at that time, both in the Irish and the English branches of the Presbyterian Church, and which, not long after his ordination, found so noble an expression in the Union, whose articles are still extant, by which the Presbyterians and Independents of England agreed to bury their distinctive names in that of UNITED BRETHREN. Willing to tolerate other denominations beside their own; readily admitting the distinction between essential and non-essential doctrines, and very far indeed from believing with their *Scotch* Presbyterian brethren, that such a distinction was itself a fundamental error; claiming no such divine authority for each peculiar shade of doctrine or discipline, as would deprive them, by a fixed and inevitable necessity, of all possible liberty of change, concession, or compromise, and wise enough to leave some matters of inferior importance to be determined by the Providence of God, we cannot be too thankful, in view of the great work that God would one day give him to do, that the young McKemie, on his first entrance upon the work of the ministry, should find himself surrounded by such a genial and invigorating atmosphere. Thoroughly qualified for his work also by a classical, a legal, and a theological education, a man of most indomitable courage and perseverance, and possessed withal of a sufficient amount of this world's goods to render him somewhat independent in his circumstances, we are not surprised to find that when an application was made to Lagan Presbytery, in Ireland, in December, 1680, for a minister to come to the Colonies, by "Col. Stevens, in Maryland, beside Virginia," that the lot should fall upon McKemie.

Arriving in 1682, and "resolving to submit himself to the sovereign Providence of God," his great aim seems to have been to preach the gospel to the destitute, and to search out localities to which he could safely invite other ministers of a similar evangelical spirit from abroad. First, within a mile of his wealthy and benevolent friend, Col. Stevens, in Somerset County, he organizes the Rehoboth Church, which is consequently the oldest Presbyterian Church, the cradle of Presbyterianism in these United States. In 1690 we find him collecting a congregation in Accomack, just on the dividing line between Virginia and Maryland. Alarmed and incensed at his evangelical labors, the Episcopal clergy carry him over the Bay to Williamsburg, to answer for the crime of preaching the gospel. But their opposition is in vain. Conciliated alike by his talents and his fascinating address, the Governor becomes his friend, gives him a general license to preach, and licenses his dwelling-house as a place of worship. Meanwhile we hear of him in Worcester County, in North Carolina, in Barbadoes, and elsewhere, with equal prudence and zeal, sowing beside all waters the good seed of the word of God. "The London Missionary Society," to which we have before alluded as "The United Brethren," or, as Dr. Miller has it, "a respectable body of Dissenters in the city of London," having ceased, after two years, to make any further appropriation for the support of their missionary, he was obliged, like Paul at Corinth, to engage in secular business. This, however, fell out rather for the furtherance of the Gospel. His business being mercantile, and himself the owner of the vessel, it was thus in his power to visit and preach in many places that he would have been obliged otherwise to neglect. Thus too it was that somewhere about the time of which we speak we find him on his way to Philadelphia.

Hitherto he has had a good reward for his labor; in spite of all the embarrassment and opposition he has been called to encounter, and that single-handed and alone, he has now under his care no less than four flourishing churches. His first anxiety is to have them supplied with a faithful and efficient MINISTRY. This makes it necessary for him to return to his native country, and to his former friends in England, to enlist anew their interest for the gospel in America. His usual success attending his application, on his voyage back he is accompanied by two fellow-laborers and fellow-countrymen, JOHN HAMPTON and GEORGE MCNISH, whom he had inspired with a portion of his own enthusiasm, and who were as little bigoted and exclusive as he was himself. The MINISTRY thus secured, and no doubt beginning to see that he was now about to lay the foundations of many generations, his next great anxiety, in order "that their evangelical affairs might be the better managed," was to organize a PRESBYTERY.

In the selection of materials for this purpose, two courses were open for his adoption. One was to stand like Jephthah and his Gileadites, at the passage of the Jordan, and cut off every Ephraimite who could not lisp the ecclesiastical shibboleth with precisely the same sibilation as himself and other Presbyterians across the water. The other was to anticipate the far reaching wisdom that afterwards prevailed with such a glorious result in our national affairs; viz. taking the elements of Presbyterianism just as he found them, to arrange, to harmonize, and to mould them afresh, in their form at least, if not their substance, after a model of his own. American Presbyterianism is no more British Presbyterianism, than American liberty is British liberty.

It was on this wise that the system was first introduced to Scotland by JOHN KNOX. "Before the common people," (the "rascal multitude," as they called them,) "had time or opportunity of being instructed or indoctrinated in the principles of the

Reformation—before there were any Sessions, or Presbyteries, or Synods instituted, a few clergymen with the nobility, formed themselves into a kind of general Assembly: planned or rather adopted, the doctrinal Confession of faith, which Knox brought with him from Geneva; seized upon the patrimony of the church, as they called it; deposed the former bishops, and appointed in their stead over their dioceses, superintendents, or a kind of itinerant bishops with very limited powers, to take the old parishes under their care, remove disorderly and immoral incumbents, locate better ministers where they could be found, over the said parishes, and where suitable ministers could not be found, to appoint readers as a temporary supply. This was according to the model established by the Scotch Reformers, and their first General Assembly. * * * All the power of the Church commenced from, and existed in a General Assembly, which organized inferior courts, when it was found expedient and necessary, and imparted to the courts below, such powers and privileges as it chose, and retained such as it chose. This system began at the top, and worked downward. It commenced in times of comparative darkness and ignorance, respecting civil and religious rights, privileges, and freedom; and becoming the established religion of the realm, it retained all the advantages thereby secured to itself, with a tenacity peculiar to the nation to the present day, to the exclusion of all other sects or denominations, excepting those in subordination to itself. It would fraternize with no other sect, admit none other into its pulpits, or church judicatories, nor open a fraternal correspondence with any other. Hence, when compelled by circumstances to attempt a union with the English Presbyterians, who were far more moderate, and less restrictive than themselves, they would not amalgamate. In New England, they wanted all their system or nothing; nothing less would satisfy them than to have Presbyterianism established there by law, to the exclusion of every other system."* The idea of preference without exclusion, was heresy.

The Father of American Presbyterianism was of a widely different spirit. Either previous to his departure from Europe, or immediately upon his return, he became acquainted with the Rev. Jedediah Andrews, who in the autumn of 1698, came from New England to Philadelphia, and officiated as an Independent minister. His congregation *then* occupying the storehouse of the Barbadoes Company, in common with the Baptists, is *now* represented by the First Presbyterian Church on Washington Square. Agreed as to their doctrine, in Calvinism: as to the sacraments, alike in their nature, mode, and subjects; as to the parity of the ministry; above all, in the noble charity of the gospel, magnifying the things in which they agreed, rather than those in which they differed, it was not difficult, it was just what we would have expected in the circumstances, that these kindred drops should mingle into one. Accordingly, A. D. 1705, McKemie and Andrews, together with Hampton, McNish, and three others, John Wilson, Samuel Davis, and Nathaniel Taylor, were organized as the mother PRESBYTERY of Philadelphia. Half of them were Irish Presbyte-

* Hill's American Presbyterianism, *passim.*

rians; the other half Congregationalists probably, and from a subsequent letter of Mr. Andrews to a friend at the East, in which he says, "that they could all submit to the Presbytery readily enough, though mostly from New England," we have as good an idea as we could desire of the *kind* of Presbyterianism that was then established. Others may call it "loose," we call it liberal. Others may denounce it as "a laxer system," we glory in it as just what it ought to have been. As one has well said, "Its connection with Scotland was slight and incidental. McKemie was Presbyterian, and he secured that form of government. Andrews was content provided it was liberal." American Presbyterianism then, was what American Presbyterianism as represented in our branch of the Church is now, AMERICAN AND NOT FOREIGN; something of its own kind, and not a mere exotic.

Our attachment to it is like that of a Jew to Palestine; both *national* and religious. We love it as we do our liberty, because it is the growth of our own soil. Presbyterianism is good, the Presbyterianism of the Waldenses in the 7th Century; the Presbyterianism of the Reformed Churches in France, Germany, Holland, Hungary, Geneva; and Scotland, apart from its individual peculiarities; to each of these we willingly accord the praise to which they are entitled by their history, and the fruits that they have borne through many generations; but for our own country, for the 19th century, for our children, and our children's children, we do most sincerely and unfeignedly believe that American Presbyterianism is better. Take away the word AMERICAN, and with it the representative principle, and the love of chartered rights as guarantied by a written constitution; make the *animus* of the Church, other than what it is now and ever has been since its original formation; give a legislative power to the General Assembly, and a discretionary power at such times as it may deem expedient, to over-ride the Constitution itself, and we would feel but little zeal to see this system established and perpetuated. The draft that the Assembly has made upon the churches, whether honored or dishonored, would be a matter of indifference to us. We would not feel as we now do, that not to have it met would be a calamity. A Church that has such an origin as we have described, should be dear alike to the heart of the patriot and the Christian.

Let us trace its *progress*. As in the formation of our National Constitution, every step of the way, from the Colonial to the State, and from the State to the General Government, the rights of the people were carefully secured by their representatives and went upward, so was it in the history of American Presbyterianism; A. D. 1717. The number of churches having greatly increased, the mother Presbytery was divided into four, and out of these the first SYNOD was constituted, viz. the Synod of New York and Philadelphia. Among other advantages secured by this arrangement was the RIGHT OF APPEAL to a higher court, viz. that of a private member from the decision of a Session and a Presbytery; and that of a minister from the decision of a Presbytery. A. D. 1788, the original Synod was divided into four, and out of the whole was constituted as the great bond of union for all the churches, the

General Assembly. Thus after four score years in building, our ecclesiastical structure was at length completed; not a Monarchy, like the Papal Church; not an oligarchy, like the Episcopal, or Methodist Episcopal; not a Democracy, like the Congregational, but a Republic. Religious rights in the Church, are secured in the same manner as civil rights in the States. The Church is the township; the Presbytery, the county; the Synod, the judicial district; the General Assembly, the congress, composed of representatives from all parts of the land. If we read aright the history of our country, and understand the working of its institutions, American Republicanism is nothing but political Presbyterianism. Those who doubt the assertion, we refer to the Mecklenburg Declaration of Independence, which anticipated that of Jefferson, and was its model; to the history of Witherspoon in the Continental Congress; and to the history of the Constitution itself.

From the *form* of American Presbyterianism, let us turn to what is of still greater importance, its *spirit*.

When after preaching the sermon in New York, A. D. 1707, (the only one still extant,) to "the small congregation," which afterwards became the First Presbyterian Church there, McKemie was arrested by Lord Cornbury, saying, "You shall not preach your pernicious doctrines here," he boldly replied, "As to our doctrines, my Lord, we have our Confession of Faith, which is known to the Christian world; and I challenge all the clergy of York to show us any false or pernicious doctrines therein." His doctrinal sentiments were undoubtedly those of the Westminster Catechism. No one will dispute his orthodoxy, though there are not a few who would in vain endeavor to conceal his liberality.

"In the organization of the Presbyterian Church in this country," says Dr. Miller, "they had not formally and publicly adopted any particular Confession of Faith, or ecclesiastical Constitution. They acted under a plan rather understood, than officially ratified."

This continued until A. D. 1729, when the question of adopting the Confession of Faith became a matter of most earnest and anxious deliberation. The points presented were the following:

1. To adhere to the Westminster Confession of Faith, Catechisms, and Directory, without the least variation or alteration, and without any regard to the distinction of essential or non-essential articles. Or,

2. Utterly "to disclaim all legislative power and authority in the church;" to leave to the discretion of the individual such articles as "were not essential or necessary in doctrine, worship, or government," and to recognize "the point of essentials and circumstantials" as an article so important as to be absolutely "indispensable."

The former was foreign Presbyterianism; the latter was American Presbyterianism; and that the latter had the preference is evident from the following minute:—

"The Synod do unanimously acknowledge and declare, that they judge the Directory for worship, discipline, and government of the Church, commonly annexed to the Westminster Confession, to be agreeable in substance to the Word of God, and founded thereupon, and therefore do earnestly recommend the same to all their members, to be by them observed as near as circumstances will allow and Christian prudence direct."

This minute, in connection with several others of similar import and spirit, known as the ADOPTING ACT, has always stood out in the history of our church, like the Declaration of Independence in the history of our nation. It is the real and only foundation on which we rest as a denomination. We want no better. The Confession of Faith *with* the Word of God, and not *instead* of or *above* it! *The essential and necessary articles of that Confession,*—this was the common ground on which the fathers met. It is still the ground of their children; first as laid down a second time in 1758, and then again by our own Assembly in 1839! Like the fabled shield, on which the heavenly smith had wrought the anticipated history of Roman glory, we see at once in this Act our protection and our dearest hopes. Let us trust the one and cherish the other.

But to illustrate still further the spirit of American Presbyterianism, take the plan of union in 1801.

Perhaps the great Head of the Church sees it best that Christendom should be broken into different communions, lest human wisdom should improve a general union to a secular use and worldly grandeur. Perhaps it may be true, according to the remark of J. J. Gurney, "that in the variety of administration, through which the saving principles of religion are permitted to pass, there is much of a real adaptation to a corresponding variety of mental condition." Be this as it may, the spirit of UNION is one with which we cannot fail to sympathize. We honor good old Duræus, who, in the seventeenth century, spent thirty years in travelling for the purpose of uniting the Protestant churches of Europe! We honor the "United Brethren," of whom we have already spoken, as actuated by a similar desire. We honor the "Evangelical Alliance," and are only sorry that its success has not been commensurate with its aim! And when we find our General Assembly in 1801 adopting regulations, "with a view to prevent alienation and promote union and harmony," and "strictly enjoining on all their missionaries to the new settlements to endeavor, by all proper means, to promote mutual forbearance and accommodation between those inhabitants who hold the Presbyterian and those who hold the Congregational form of government," we honor *them*. Stript of all the peculiarities, which externally separate them from one another, we are bound, in the exercise of that charity that never faileth, to love all whom Christ loves; where the difference is little to make it still less; and, where it is possible so to do, to merge it altogether. The spirit of McKemie at the beginning; of the adopting act in 1729, and of the plan of union in 1801, is one of which we need never to be ashamed.

True, the history of this plan has been somewhat of the strangest! What was intended to promote external union has, at length, divided us among ourselves. Our brethren of the other branch of the Church abrogated it because it promoted Congregationalism. On the other hand, our Congregational brethren have withdrawn from it because it favored Presbyterianism. Meanwhile we, who have stood by the covenant of our fathers, through evil report and good report, and have suffered the loss of all things for its sake, have yet this comfort left, that Francis had at the battle of Pavia, "We have lost all but honor." We believe that our fathers were right, and that what we lose now by imitating their example, we shall gain in the future.

Wickedness is always weak,
But truth is young and strong.

The last illustration we adduce of the spirit of American Presbyterianism, is one that we by no means present with the least pleasure. The test question, and one that will alone determine in the eyes of the nation, whether they are worthy of the name of *American* Presbyterians, is, where were they in 1776? In answering for the clergy, we answer for the people, also, whose hearts, and the hearts of their people were as one in the matter of the Revolution. Not with the Methodist clergy, who in obedience to ecclesiastical authority, had either withdrawn from the country, or remained only to observe a strict neutrality. "We are no Republicans," said Mr. Wesley, "and never intend to be!" Not with the Episcopal clergy! "As a body, the Episcopalians of the country were either openly or covertly devoted to the English interest, and great numbers of their clergy resigned their charges and went home in disgust, while those who remained as a general thing, both preached and prayed against the cause of the Colonies." *Thompson's reply to Schuyler*, p. 266.

Not with enemies, or neutrals, were Presbyterians

to be found, but heart and hand, and soul, with their Congregational brethren of New England for liberty, and against oppression! The name of the martyred Caldwell, and many a chaplain on the rolls of the revolutionary army, and of those who officiated in the old Continental Congress, through all the times that tried men's souls, will tell you *where!* So also will the sermons then preached and still extant; the heavy rewards offered for their heads by the British governors; the confidential letters of Washington, who depended much on them for information by which to carry out his plans; the well-known hostility of the invading army which, as in the case of the old Pine Street Church of this city, almost invariably destroyed every parsonage in which they lived, every edifice in which they worshipped! And more than all, the mightier weapon than any named in war, that they were enabled to wield, the ministerial prayer meeting, which they established for the especial purpose of imploring the blessing of the God of armies, upon their country, in her great struggle for independence; these things will show the value and efficiency of the support which they rendered at that eventful period. "There," said one of them, whose name is attached to the Declaration of Independence, and who thus addressed his fellow patriots: "There stands the widow of my dear Henry, and these his orphan children. His brother died bravely by his side, fighting for freedom. But God knows my heart! I had rather all my remaining sons should fall in the field of battle as their brothers fell, than see the noble cause now surrendered. By the graves of your fathers, who on this ground withstood and conquered the wild and ferocious Indians—by the love of your mothers, divinely preserved from the war-club, the scalping knife, the tomahawk—by the purity and honor of your daughters, your sisters, your wives, now threatened with rapine and pollution—by the hope of unborn posterity, for whom chains and fetters are now clanking in your ears —by the authority, and in the name of the great God, who has said the world shall be free, I beseech, I conjure you arouse! Rush to sustain the Eagle of Liberty while yet it flies! Let the mother say to her son, Go, and God be with you. Let the wife encourage her husband! Let the sister cheer, animate, urge her brothers to go where honor, religion, and their country call. These gray hairs must soon descend into the sepulchre; yet I would infinitely rather they should descend thither by the hands of the public executioner, than desert at this crisis, the sacred cause of my country!" It was this same man, who in 1788, reported the original Constitution of our Church, which was not only adopted the same year as our National Constitution; but to which the latter is largely indebted as its model. Piety will have died out of the Church, and patriotism out of the land, when the name of WITHERSPOON is forgotten.

To praise such men as these, if that were all, were an easy matter. *Virtus laudatur et alget.* "The true way of testifying our respect and love for the departed," says a Roman annalist, "is not to follow them with an unavailing grief, but to remember their wishes and fulfil their injunctions." The Church that they commenced in the midst of persecutions, and established while the smoke was yet rising from the crimsoned field of war, is not yet obsolete. Dear for all the memories of the past, growing with the growth, and strengthening with the strength of our common country, it still retains its original form; it breathes the same liberal spirit; it is equally worthy of present support, and future enlargement. As God has made the debt of love we owe him, payable to our fellow men, so we owe a debt to our ancestry, equalled in magnitude only by that which we owe to posterity, and in a similar manner, made payable to *them*. Serving our day and generation, according to the highest style of meaning to be attached to this expression, we are to live for the world, and for all coming time! How to do this is an easy problem. The best way to live for the world, is to live for our country, and to adopt as our motto, "Our country for the sake of the world." The best way to live for our country, is to live for the Church. The family, the State, and the Church, these are God's institutions, whatever man's may be; and only as these are maintained can society be perpetuated, defended and sanctified. The best way to live for the Church as a whole, is to live for that particular portion of it where God has cast our lot. Neutrals *in* the Church, like neutrals out of it, are too often if reports are true, like the combined fleets at present under the walls of Constantinople, they are *there*, but what good do they do!

For our own part, we love the American Presbyterian Church in these United States, because we love our country, and the Church universal. Holding as we do nine out of twelve essential doctrines of truth and order in common with every evangelical denomination, the difference between us and the Methodists is, that we put God first, and not second in the order of salvation: between us and the Episcopalian, the parity of the clergy; we do not believe in Lords over God's heritage; between us and the Baptist, that we come into the Church not as individuals, but as families: between us and the Congregationalist, that we wish a CONSTITUTION to protect our rights, and not have them subject to the mere will of a majority: between us and the brethren of the other branch of the Presbyterian Church, whether we shall take the Confession of Faith as Edwards was willing to take it for "substance of doctrine," as it was introduced by McKemie, adopted in 1729, re-adopted in 1758, and held by Davies and others, or whether we shall hold it to be the very pattern showed in the mount, sentence for sentence, word for word, and letter for letter, except for purposes of excision. Or to state this matter as it has been well stated by another, "Whether a man should be executed before he is tried, or tried before he is executed!" We glory in the things in which we agree with other evangelical denominations; we are not ashamed of those in which we differ.

Pardon, in this connection, another allusion; (for sometimes out of the fullness of the heart the mouth will speak.) We love this portion of the Presbyterian Church, which one day, we trust, will have the name of the AMERICAN PRESBYTERIAN Church, as it already has *the thing*, because it has been slandered, greatly slandered, deliberately and perseveringly slandered by those who have cast out our name as evil, and said, Let the Lord be glorified. To be reproached as bigots by infidels, is nothing more than we might expect of those whose hatred of religion is in exact proportion to its purity. The accusations of fatalism, infant damnation, and such like caricatures of Calvinism, we can readily pardon on the score of ignorance in those that make them; but to be told, and have all the world told, in print, and that stereotyped, and published edition after edition, that we believe what we do not believe, that we do not believe what we *do*, in reference to such fundamental doctrines of the gospel as depravity, atonement, and regeneration by the Holy Ghost, is now, and always has been, considered by us a matter so unkind, so ungenerous, so utterly unlike everything we have a right to expect of those who *ought* to know us better, that if we should undertake to express our feelings on this subject, we would not know where to begin; if we began, where to end. Only thus much we will say,—call it perversity, a sense of justice, a law of moral compensation, or what you will, just in proportion as our beloved church has thus been covered with obloquy, misrepresentation, and contempt, have we learned to love her more, for Christ's sake, and to appreciate her real merits for her own.

But the days of our ecclesiastical mourning seem about to end. Lo! the winter is past, the rain is over and gone, the flowers appear on the earth, the time of the singing of birds is come, and the voice of the turtle is heard in our land! This very 100,000 dollars that is demanded, and on all hands admitted to be so greatly needed, is an evidence, than which we want none better, that our condition is not that of a denomination that decayeth and dieth away. The necessity for an increased expenditure is an index of prosperity in temporal affairs: why is it not also a mark of the divine favor in spiritual? More capital is only wanted, when more of it can be employed to good advantage; or, to change the figure, "It is a maxim in the military art," said Napoleon, "that the army which remains in its entrenchments is beaten." We are glad to see that the maxim is likely to have no application in reference to us, for we are now upon the *advance!*

"Walk about Zion, and go round about her: tell the towers thereof. Mark ye well her bulwarks, consider her palaces; that ye may tell it to the generation following!"

Look at the increase of our church since 1837! In Synods, 63 per cent.; in Presbyteries, 56 per cent.; in churches, 42 per cent.; in communicants, 74 per cent.; in licentiates, 47 per cent.

Look at her schools of the prophets in New York, Auburn, Cincinnati, Maryville.

Look at her relative position in such States as New York, Pennsylvania, Ohio, Michigan, New Jersey, Illinois, Tennessee; and superiority in such cities as New York, Philadelphia, Washington, Buffalo, Detroit, Chicago!

Look at her government, so perfectly in harmony and sympathy with the government of these United States!

Look at her principles: those that have withstood the test of ages elsewhere, and are now reproduced in a form in which they will last for ages to come; and doubt, if you can, that this is a plant which the Lord hath planted, and which shall not be rooted up!

It may be an error, my brethren; it may be one of those day-dreams that pass away, just in proportion as our shadows lengthen and our sun declines, but the delusion is, at least, a pleasant one while it lasts, and is in our heart of hearts too deep to be willingly abandoned,—that American Presbyterians, purified seven times, as they have been in the crucible of God's mysterious providence, are one day to have a name and a place, nobly pre-eminent among the tribes of our national Israel! and that they, who once said to the man of God, whose memory still hallows these walls,* and whose crown shines so resplendent in heaven, "We do not know you, sir," and sent him home, with a broken heart, to die; will find that the NATION does! that God has made the wrath of man to praise him, and the remainder thereof he has restrained.

Even now, methinks, I catch the not far distant strain, "O! thou afflicted, tossed with tempest and not comforted, behold I will lay thy stones with fair colors, and lay thy foundations with sapphires. And I will make thy windows of agate, and thy gates of carbuncles, and all thy borders of pleasant stones. And all thy children shall be taught of the Lord, and great shall be the peace of thy children. In righteousness shalt thou be established: thou shalt be far from oppression, for thou shalt not fear, and from terror, for it shall not come near thee."

* REV. JAMES PATTERSON, in whose church this sermon was repeated.

www.ingramcontent.com/pod-product-compliance
Lightning Source LLC
LaVergne TN
LVHW011143110826
845150LV00008B/2481
* 9 7 8 1 4 1 8 1 9 2 8 5 3 *